Clothed in Majesty

European Ecclesiastical Textiles from the Detroit Institute of Arts

Peter Barnet

Clothed in Majesty

The Detroit Institute of Arts

This catalogue accompanies the exhibition "Clothed in Majesty: European Ecclesiastical Textiles from the Detroit Institute of Arts," September 14, 1991— February 9, 1992.

The exhibition is supported by the National Endowment for the Arts, the Visiting Committee for European Sculpture and Decorative Arts, the city of Detroit, the State of Michigan, and the Founders Society Detroit Institute of Arts.

Cover: Shield, cat. no. 15

Foreword

The collection of European textiles and costumes in the Detroit Institute of Arts consists of over fifteen thousand pieces. Developed by textile scholar Adele Coulin Weibel during her years as curator and curator emeritus (1927-1963), it ranks among the most important such collections in the United States. Since Mrs. Weibel's retirement this significant collection has been without a curatorial specialist and, as a result, it is too little known and infrequently exhibited.

The European ecclesiastical textiles selected for *Clothed in Majesty* represent the major forms of vestments used in the western Catholic tradition, such as copes, dalmatics, and chasubles, as well as some pieces from the Eastern Church. Also included are orphreys, stoles, maniples, altar frontals, a chalice veil, and a lectern cover, representing a variety of forms, materials, and techniques and ranging in date from circa 1100 to circa 1850. Some of the textiles exhibited were acquired in the earliest days of the museum's history before Mrs. Weibel's tenure, but most represent purchases she made; also included are some important recent acquisitions. A number of little-known masterpieces of unsurpassed quality will thus get a rare showing.

I would like to acknowledge the expertise and hard work of Peter Barnet, Associate Curator of European Sculpture and Decorative Arts, in organizing this exhibition and catalogue. We are also very grateful to the Visiting Committee which supports that department and to the National Endowment for the Arts for their grants.

Samuel Sachs II
Director

Acknowledgments

I am greatly indebted to Alice Zrebiec, Associate Curator of European Sculpture and Decorative Arts, Metropolitan Museum of Art, New York, who was a National Endowment for the Arts Visiting Specialist at the Detroit Institute of Arts from 1983-87. During that time she studied the European ecclesiastical textiles in the collection and the exhibition is a direct outgrowth of her excellent work. Angela Lakwete, Textile Conservator at the Detroit Institute of Arts (1985-90), greatly facilitated this study and subsequently reviewed the materials and techniques of each piece and prepared many of the pieces for installation. The exhibition and catalogue would not have been possible without the insight and generosity of these two dedicated textile specialists. Any errors, however, are my own responsibility.

Others who provided valuable assistance to the project are Constancio del Alamo, the Reverend Duane Arnold, Tina Takayanagi Barnet, Mollie Fletcher, Géza Jászai, Nobuko Kajitani, Dorothy Kostuch, Edward Maeder, Susan Madigan, Christa C. Mayer-Thurman, Mrs. William J. Robertson, and Janet Whitson.

Many members of the museum staff deserve thanks for their efforts on behalf of the exhibition. The project was encouraged from the outset by Samuel Sachs II, Director; Jan van der Marck, Chief Curator; Alan P. Darr, Curator of European Sculpture and Decorative Arts; and Tara Robinson, Curator, Exhibition Coordination. The excellent photography was taken under often trying conditions, principally by Robert Hensleigh, Associate Director of Photography. Barbara Heller, Head Conservator, James Leacock, Mount Design Fabricator, and Louis Gauci, Group Director, Exhibitions and Design, contributed greatly to the exhibition. Jane K. Hutchins of Tideview Conservation expertly prepared some of the pieces for installation. The installation crew, as always, deserve special credit for their careful handling of the fragile textiles. Patience Young, Curator of Education, Jennifer Williams, Curatorial Assistant, and Sarah Deitch, intern in the Education Department, helped with the education program. Jennifer Hill, intern in the Exhibition Coordination department, helped with the glossary and the educational materials for the exhibition. Julia Henshaw, Director of Publications, and Opal Suddeth-Hodge, Executive Secretary, were of great assistance in finalizing the catalogue, which was sensitively designed by Jan Z. Cohen. Bonita LaMarche, Assistant Curator, and Lissa Roos, Senior Typist, both in the European Sculpture and Decorative Arts department, graciously offered valuable assistance and much-appreciated encouragement.

I would also like to thank the Visiting Committee for European Sculpture and Decorative Arts for their support of this catalogue. The National Endowment for the Arts contributed greatly to the project, initially with the Visiting Specialist grant and later with a grant directly supporting the exhibition.

Peter Barnet
Associate Curator of European Sculpture and Decorative Arts

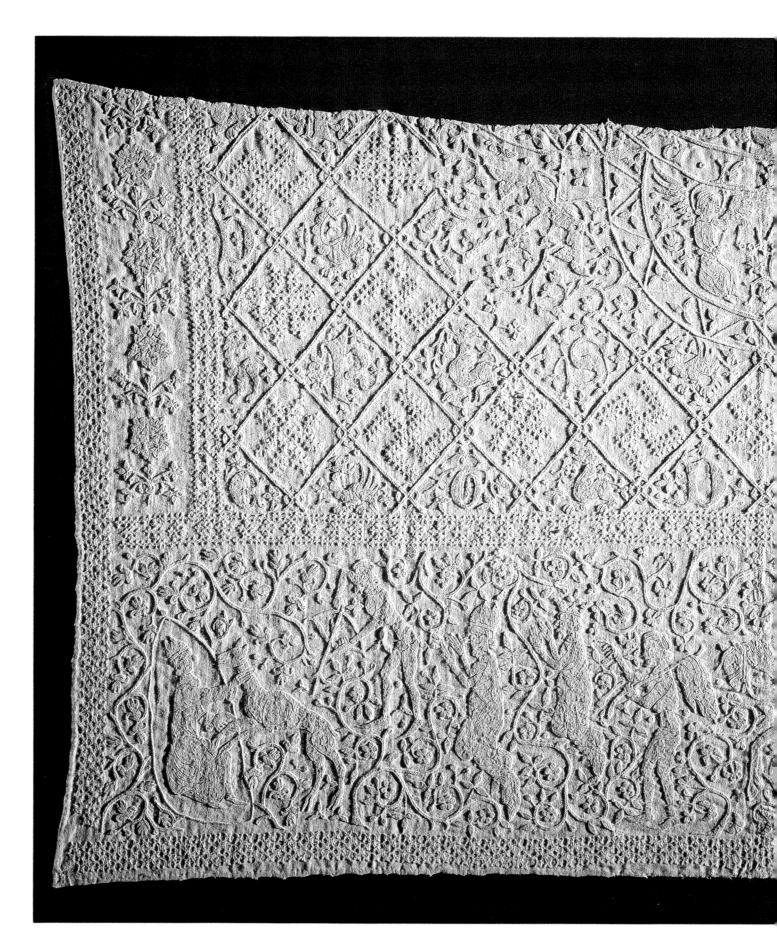

✳ 3

✳ 18

Clothed in Majesty

Museums exhibit countless precious works of art used in Christian worship throughout the history of the church. Eucharistic vessels such as chalices and patens of gold, silver, and enamel, for instance, are familiar to museum visitors, as are crosses, croziers, and reliquaries. The garments worn by the clergy and the textiles used to cover the altar, and the surrounding furniture, are no less precious than the more familiar gold and silver vessels. Because of their fragile nature, however, fewer textiles have survived, particularly from the early periods. The examples we are fortunate to have preserved are usually carefully stored away from damaging light, and consequently away from public view.

During the Middle Ages and the Renaissance, vestments and other ecclesiastical textiles were often richly embroidered with Christian imagery in silk, gold, and silver thread. Later, during the Baroque and Rococo periods, it became more common in the church to use patterned silk fabrics without Christian imagery. Many of these seventeenth- and eighteenth-century textiles were originally woven for secular use and were passed on to the church when they were no longer at the height of fashion. Taste and style changed in the church as well as in secular culture, but the essentially conservative nature of the church preserved many of the textile treasures we have today.

When conducting religious services, members of the clergy wear garments appropriate to their position and function in the liturgy. These garments and insignia, such as the crozier, are known collectively as vestments (see glossary). The most complete sets of matching vestments include two dalmatics, two chasubles, a mitre for a bishop, two stoles, two maniples, and a cope. An antependium, a chalice veil, a chalice cover, and a burse are also all sometimes part of a set.

Two fundamental ecclesiastical garments which rarely survive and are not represented in the exhibition are the amice and the alb, both usually made of white linen. The amice is a rectangular cloth worn around the neck and shoulders by nearly all clergy. It is usually the first garment to be put on. By the twelfth century the alb was regularly worn by all priests, deacons, and bishops beneath their vestments. Other clerics, such as acolytes and subdeacons, wear the alb as an outer garment. The alb is long-sleeved and ankle-length. Decorative panels called apparels, usually embroidered, are often applied to the amice and to the alb just above the hem at the front and back and at the cuffs.

The principal vestment of deacons, the lowest order of clergy, is the dalmatic, a shin-length tunic with sleeves, allowing the apparels of the alb worn beneath to show. Dalmatics are usually made of silk. Decorative orphrey bands, sometimes called clavi, run vertically from the shoulders to the hem on many dalmatics. Others have orphrey panels across the chest or above the hem.

✴ *14*

Priests and bishops wear the dalmatic beneath the chasuble, which is their principal garment. As the outer vestment for the priest officiating at the Eucharist, or celebrant, the chasuble had to be made of silk and is often richly decorated with embroidered orphreys. Before the twelfth century, the chasuble was essentially conical in shape. By the sixteenth century, however, the chasuble had evolved into a vestment split at the sides, as in all of the examples in the exhibition.

The stole is a narrow strip of cloth worn under the dalmatic or chasuble, hanging down nearly to the ankles. The deacon wears the stole on the left shoulder, the priest crosses it over the chest, and the bishop wears it around the back of the neck hanging straight down the front. The maniple is a shorter strip of cloth worn by most clergy over the left forearm.

✳ 25

Priests and higher clergy wear copes as processional vestments. This semi-circular cloak is worn over the shoulders and fastened in front with a morse — often an elaborate brooch, but sometimes simply a cloth strap. Copes are frequently decorated with an orphrey band running along the straight edge and a purely decorative shield or hood at the back of the neck. This developed from the original function of the cope as an outer garment designed to protect the wearer against the weather.

✳ 1, 2

✳ 1, 2, 5
✳ 3,4

Church vestments evolved slowly in the early Christian period and in the early Middle Ages. Forms were originally derived from late Roman dress and they were not strictly regularized until about the twelfth century, a time of reform in the church. The earliest pieces in the exhibition date roughly from this period of reform. All five of the western medieval textiles in the exhibition are fragmentary, but the three woven textiles and the two Germanic embroideries suggest the considerable range of the medieval achievement in textiles.

✳ 3

✳ 19, 20

The fourteenth-century Westphalian embroidered lectern cover is relatively large at more than two feet high and four feet wide, but the entire cover was probably at least six times that length. The term "lectern cover" is somewhat misleading. In fact, the embroidery would have covered a stand for a large choir book such as a missal. German white-on-white embroidery was traditionally done by nuns and the lectern cover is probably the product of a convent. The two sixteenth-century Swiss embroideries on white linen represent the end of this Germanic tradition, although it is not likely that either of them come from a monastic context.

✳ 4

The lectern cover is a rare example of its kind and it is highly sophisticated in its use of a variety of stitches to create a subtle pictorial relief. The use of linen and the absence of color, however, are in keeping with the monastic context. The elegant embroidery of the Bohemian orphrey in silk and metallic thread, in contrast, represents the highest level of professional embroidery at a time when Prague was a major cultural center of Europe. Indeed, the delicacy and lyrical quality of the *Crucifixion* on the back of this chasuble is consistent with the so-called International Style that was pervasive in all the arts across Europe around 1400.

The western tradition of decorating vestments with Christian imagery, often embroidered in silk and metallic thread, began in the Middle Ages and continued during the Renaissance. With the manufacture of purely ornamental silks in the Baroque period, however, the western tradition dissipated.

Beginning in the Early Christian period, the Byzantine church developed its own visual vocabulary. The eastern tradition of embroidery endured long after the fall of Constantinople to the Turks in 1453. The Russian banner, for example, presents an exotic combination of textiles. The Byzantine image of the *Deesis* is embroidered as the focal point, with later woven silk pendants and a Central Asian ikat lining. The Georgian *Epitaphios* conveys the richness of eastern embroidery on a monumental scale. The large areas of fine silk embroidery, in fact, can easily be mistaken for appliqués.

✳ *6-8*
✳ *7*

✳ *8*

Western orphreys were not always embroidered. The Cologne border, for example is a late medieval example of a woven orphrey, and it was probably a less expensive alternative to embroidered panels. The exhibition also includes four Italian orphrey panels woven in silk. The indebtedness of the imagery in these orphreys to Florentine painting of the fifteenth century has resulted in the traditional attribution to Florence for such textiles. Siena and Lucca, however, are also likely places of manufacture, and, in the absence of detailed information about workshops, it is wise to think of a general attribution to Tuscany for these Renaissance textiles.

✳ *5*

✳ *9-12*

The greatest strength of the museum's collection of ecclesiastical textiles lies in embroidered pieces from the fifteenth and sixteenth centuries. While the fourteenth-century German lectern cover was probably embroidered by nuns, records indicate that by 1300 Parisian embroiderers were already organized into craft guilds. By the fifteenth century monastic production was rare, and embroiderers throughout Europe belonged to guilds, with membership in nearly all cases restricted to men. In some large centers there were specialized embroiderers' guilds, but more frequently the embroiderers were grouped with other related artisans such as painters and sculptors. The church was the major patron for embroidery during this period, but by the seventeenth century private patronage had become increasingly important.

✳ *13-18*

Ecclesiastical embroidery on garments was generally confined to apparels and orphrey panels. The vertical orphreys of the dalmatic are the narrowest areas and they are often decorated with standing figures of saints, which lend themselves well to the format. The orphreys of chasubles and copes, as well as the shields of copes, provide larger surfaces for embroidered images, and scenes from the Life of Christ and the Life of the Virgin are common there. Other themes, such as the Seven Sacraments, which appears on the orphreys and shield from a cope formerly in the collection of the Duke of Arenberg, are exceedingly rare.

✳ *15*

✳ 14

The production of embroidery was a complex industry at the end of the Middle Ages and in the Renaissance. High-quality work was produced in many areas, but there was a concentration of production in the Netherlands, which became known for the export of ecclesiastical embroidery. It is common to find Netherlandish embroidery in silk and metallic thread combined with luxurious textiles woven elsewhere, such as the Italian velvet of the dalmatic. Embroiderers generally relied on designs or patterns made by someone else, occasionally well-known artists. Patterns could easily be carried by designers or embroiderers from place to place, and they were often copied, complicating specific attributions to individual workshops, and even to specific centers. The pattern, embroidery, and fabric for a garment could come from three different locations to be assembled ultimately by a tailor elsewhere.

✳ 21, 22

Tapestry weaving was also a major textile industry at the end of the Middle Ages, although it was more often associated with secular rather than ecclesiastical decoration. The Netherlands was preeminent in tapestry production and export as it was in embroidery. Tapestry was not used to decorate garments, but it frequently appeared in churches in the form of altar frontals, hangings above choir stalls, and a variety of other wall decorations.

✳ 23-34

Thus, the exhibition conveys the range of European textiles produced from about 1100 through the Middle Ages, the Renaissance, and the Baroque period. Although there are few examples of embroidery and little ecclesiastical imagery found in textiles after about 1600, the remaining pieces in the exhibition, dating mostly from the seventeenth and eighteenth centuries, can be seen as a part of the continuing history of European textile design, particularly in silk weaving. By the seventeenth century silk patterns changed rapidly in response to fashion and in some instances silks were undoubtedly passed on to the church as new styles emerged. It would, however, be incorrect to assume that the church acquired only unwanted or second-hand fabrics. There is often little or no distinction between secular and ecclesiastical fabrics and it is likely that the church was a significant customer for Baroque and Rococo silks — if not the dominant force it had been earlier in the demand for luxurious textiles.

European Ecclesiastical Textiles
from the Detroit Institute of Arts

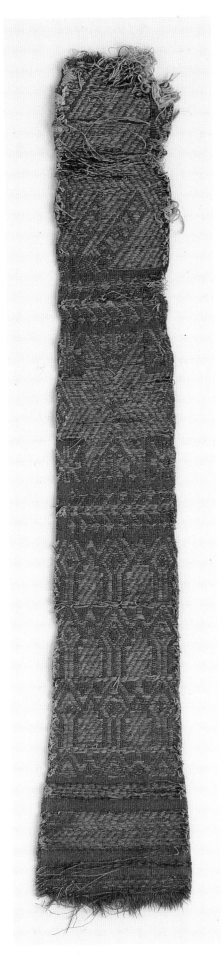

✳ 1

Lappet

German; 12/13th century
Tablet weaving: silk with
supplementary metallic
thread
16½ x 3 in.
(41.9 x 7.6 cm)
Founders Society Purchase,
Octavia W. Bates Fund
(50.37)

Provenance:
Bardini collection, Florence;
Adolph Loewi, Los Angeles;
Joseph Brummer, New York;
Disegni, New York; Adolph
Loewi, Los Angeles

Publications:
Parke-Bernet Galleries 1949,
no. 530; Weibel 1952, no. 186

Exhibitions:
Cranbrook 1965

The use of red silk and gold thread,
as well as the geometric pattern of
this mitre streamer, suggest the
boldness of medieval weaving of the
Romanesque period. Tablet weaving, done without a loom, can be
used for the creation of wider fabrics,
but it is a technique particularly
well suited to the creation of narrow
bands such as this lappet. The use
of supplementary, brocaded metallic
thread makes this lappet more elaborate than many other examples of
the period. In the Joseph Brummer
sale of 1949 this was one of a pair of
lappets attached to a mitre made
of fourteenth-century silk. The
Museum of Fine Arts, Boston, has
the mate to this lappet (50.7).

On medieval tablet weaving, see
Battiscombe 1956 and Müller-
Christensen 1977; on the technique
of tablet weaving and the use of
brocading, see Collingwood 1982.

✳ 2

Cope Fragment

Northern Spain (Burgos?);
13th century
Samit (twill with inner warp
and complementary weft):
linen, silk, and metallic
thread
6 x 18¼ in.
(15.2 x 46.3 cm)
Founders Society Purchase,
Octavia W. Bates Fund
(46.313)

Provenance:
Sangiorgi collection, Rome;
Adolph Loewi, Los Angeles
Publications:
Weibel 1952, no. 189
Exhibitions:
Cranbrook 1965

This horizontal fragment has a row
of four medallions within hexagons,
each enclosing a pair of addorsed
lions. It is one of many similar
fragments in Europe and in the
United States remaining from the
cope of Abbot Arnaldo Ramón de
Biure (d. 1351) of San Cugat de
Vallés near Barcelona. Although
ascribed by Weibel and others to a
German workshop in Regensburg,
technical evidence and the presence
of pseudo-Kufic inscriptions in some
of the fragments argue for a Spanish
origin. The fragments of the Biure
cope have much in common with
silk textiles found in 1944 in the
royal tombs at Las Huelgas in
Burgos and the design of the Biure
fragments is consistent with Mudéjar
art of the thirteenth century, which
assimilated much of the art of the
Islamic south of Spain. For further
information, see Shepherd 1951 and
May 1957.

*Fragment of a
Lectern Cover*
German (Westphalia);
1350/1400
Embroidery: linen on linen
plain weave
27¼ x 49⅛ in.
(69 x 125 cm)
Founders Society Purchase,
Robert H. Tannahill
Foundation Fund with a
contribution from the David
L. Klein, Jr., Memorial
Foundation
(1989.47)

Provenance:
Hillemeyer collection,
Paderborn, Germany;
European art market

Publications:
Aldenkirchen 1884; Ludorff
1899; Gräbke 1938; Einhorn
1971; Einhorn 1976; *BDIA*,
vol. 65, no. 4, 1990, p. 56.

This linen embroidery is one end of a lectern cover, which originally could have been as long as fourteen feet. The frieze-like border depicts an episode from the life of Saint Giles (or Aegidius, d. ca. 710) who, according to legend, lived as a hermit in a cave near the Rhône river in France. When a hind pursued by a royal hunting party sought shelter with Giles, the hermit was accidentally wounded by an arrow. He refused medical attention but was miraculously healed, inspiring the king to found a monastery on the spot, known today as Saint-Gilles-du-Gard in Provence. The embroidery depicts the saint in his cave at the left as the king and bishop, both on horseback, approach from the right with the hunters. The arc at the top center of the textile, which enframes two winged angels, is the bottom lobe of a quatrefoil. Most of the remainder of the piece is occupied by a field with a lattice ground decorated with delicately drawn ornamental motifs including dragons, swasticas, and Gothic initials.

Based on similarities in design, it is likely that the remainder of this embroidery closely resembled the nearly complete lectern cover in the Wiesenkirche in Soest, Westphalia (Gräbke 1938, fig. 85 [sic]). One end of the Soest cover illustrates the same episode from the life of Saint Giles while at the opposite end is a second frieze-like border depicting the Adoration of the Magi. Between the two narrative borders of the Soest piece are three fields each dominated by a central quatrefoil.

White-on-white embroideries of this type are associated with Westphalian workmanship in the Gothic period. Comparison with the Soest lectern cover and other extant pieces of white-on-white embroidery, as well as such evidence as the costumes of the figures in this piece, suggest that it should be dated to the second half of the fourteenth century.

see fold-out on p. 5

detail

#4

Back of a Chasuble

Bohemian orphrey ca. 1400,
on 15th-century Italian
velvet
Orphrey embroidery: silk,
and metallic thread on linen
plain weave; Velvet: silk
43³/₄ x 25 in.
(111.1 x 63.5 cm)
Gift of Mr. and Mrs. Leslie
H. Green, Bloomfield Hills,
Michigan
(46.1)

Provenance:
Adolph Loewi, Venice; Jules
S. Bache, New York; Adolph
Loewi, Los Angeles

Publications:
Kende Galleries 1945,
no. 362; Weibel 1946

Exhibitions:
Michigan State University
1968; Detroit 1978, checklist
no. 23

The cut and voided velvet that forms
this somewhat worn chasuble back is
characteristic of Italian silk weaving
of the fifteenth century. The chasuble, however, is somewhat shorter
and narrower than usual for the fifteenth century, suggesting either
that the vestment has been cut down
at a later date or that the velvet was
not originally used for the vestment.

The embroidery of the orphrey panels is in good condition, although it is readily apparent that it has been cut down at top and bottom. Furthermore, the arms of Christ and of the cross have been removed from their original ground and sewn onto the flanking horizontal sections with figures of the prophets. It is possible that the orphrey was originally Y-shaped, a disposition found in Bohemian chasubles of the late Gothic period (similar chasubles in the collegiate church at Rokycany near Pilsen and in the abbey at Broumov are illustrated in Drobná 1950).

Christ is shown crucified on a Y-shaped cross surmounted by the letters *INRI*. An angel collects the blood issuing from Christ's side in a chalice while the Virgin and Saint John mourn below Christ's feet and Mary Magdalene kneels at the base of the cross. The graceful style of the superb embroidery of the *Crucifixion* can be compared to many other Bohemian products of the period around 1400. The region was a political and cultural capital of Europe during and after the reign of Emperor Charles IV (1346-1378). On the art and culture of Bohemia in the late Gothic period, see Cologne 1978 (esp. vol. 2, pp. 585-774).

✳ 5

Orphrey

German (Cologne);
15th century
Samit (twill with inner warp and complementary weft):
silk, bast, and metallic thread
37 x 2³/₄ in.
(94 x 7 cm)
Founders Society Purchase, Octavia W. Bates Fund
(70.906)

Provenance:
Loewi-Robertson Inc., Los Angeles

This woven orphrey is characteristic of so-called Cologne borders of the fifteenth century. The inscriptions *IHESUS* and *MARIA* alternate between a flowering tree, a fruit-laden tree, and an *M* within a garland. This example is similar to the orphreys added in the eighteenth or nineteenth century to the chasuble of Saint Anno (ca. 1010-75), Archbishop of Cologne, now in the Schnütgen Museum in Cologne. On the Anno chasuble, see Chicago 1975 (no. 1) and Scheyer 1932.

✳ 6
Roundel from a Vestment

Greek(?); 15/16th century
Embroidery: silk and
metallic thread on linen
plain weave
Diameter 4³/₄ in. (12.1 cm)
Gift of Mrs. Albert Kahn,
Detroit
(29.37)

Provenance:
Leopold Iklé, St. Gall,
Switzerland; Arnold
Seligman, New York and Paris

Publications:
Zurich 1923 no. 767, pl. 137,
p. 100; *BDIA*, vol. 10, no. 6,
1929, p. 81

This embroidered roundel depicts
the half-length Christ with both
hands raised in blessing. He has a
cruciform nimbus and the rounded
mitre (*mitra*) of the Eastern Church.
He wears a *phelonion*, equivalent to
the western chasuble; an *omophorion*
worn by bishops, crossed at the
neck; a ceremonial cloth called an
epigonation, a ceremonial hand-
kerchief similar to the western
maniple, across the stomach; and
cuffs known as *epimanikia*.

✳ 7
Banner

Russian; 16th century
Embroidery: silk and
metallic thread on silk satin
Overall 45 x 22¹/₄ in.
(114.3 x 56.5 cm),
embroidered panel
21¹/₄ x 18³/₄ in.
(54 x 48 cm)
Gift of Mr. and Mrs. Joseph
B. Schlotman, Grosse
Pointe, Michigan
(25.209)

Publications:
Weibel 1927

The banner is composed of three
distinct textiles. The embroidery is
Russian, most likely from the sixteenth century. The pendants are of
a woven floral-patterned silk dating
from the eighteenth or nineteenth
century. The predominantly red
silk and cotton ikat lining seen at the
top of the banner is a central Asian
textile of the nineteenth century.

The embroidery in silk and metallic
thread on a red silk satin ground depicts the *Deesis*, or Christ the Judge,
enthroned, holding an open Gospel
Book, flanked by the Virgin and
Saint John the Baptist standing in
prayer. The side and bottom borders
are composed of seraphim alternat-
ing with a cross inscribed in a
blossom. The top border has a cross
within a circle. The inscriptions
identify Christ, Saint John, and
Mary, as "most holy mother of God."
The image of the *Deesis* and the style
of the vestments is indebted to earlier Byzantine art, but the Russian
embroidery likely dates from the sixteenth century. On the embroidery
of the Eastern Church in general,
see Millet 1947 and Johnstone 1967.

✳ 8

Epitaphios Sindon

Georgian (USSR); 17th century
Embroidery: silk and metallic thread on silk plain weave
41³/₄ x 74 in.
(106 x 188 cm)
Gift of Mr. and Mrs. James O. Keene, Birmingham, Michigan
(53.476)

Publications:
Weibel 1954-55

Exhibitions:
St. Petersburg 1967; Detroit 1978, checklist no. 34

The *Epitaphios Sindon* is used in the Eastern Church only once a year, from Good Friday until Easter, as a cover for the ceremonial bier of Christ. While the image of the dead body of Christ is always central to an *Epitaphios*, the surrounding imagery varies somewhat.

In this example Christ is flanked by the standing figures of the mourning Virgin and Saint John. Between them in the upper half of the *Epitaphios* are Saint Michael, the Annunciation to the Virgin, Saint Martha, and Saint Joseph. Below the body is an angel with a flabellum (liturgical fan) and the angel and a woman at the empty tomb. Also in the central field are seraphim, stars, and symbolic thrones (winged wheels). The symbols of the four Evangelists appear in the corners. The inscriptions that identify the figures as well as the dedicatory inscription around the borders are written in Khutsuri, an ecclesiastical Georgian alphabet. The dedicatory inscription can be translated:

With the help of God, I sinner Ikakhtha, daughter of King Khosro, Elene having become Ekaterine, wife of Messire Pharsdan of Phanaskert, have undertaken to adorn the Holy Descent from the cross of Christ our God, for the ransom of the souls of our family; to obtain a long life for our sons and daughters, my daughter, the nun Anastasia, has designed and embroidered this (Descent). Help and pity us, Holy Christ. Amen.

For other surviving examples of *Epitaphios Sindon*, see Johnstone 1967, pp. 117-28; Gurdus 1969, and Théocharis 1977.

✳ 9

Orphrey Fragment

Italian (Tuscany); 1450/1500
Lampas: silk and metallic
thread
47$^{1}/_{2}$ x 8$^{7}/_{8}$ in.
(120.6 x 22.5 cm)
City of Detroit Purchase
(19.142.0)

Provenance:
Sangiorgi Galleries, New York

Publications:
Weibel 1937; *BDIA*, vol. 1, no.
5, 1920, p. 78

Exhibitions:
Muskegon 1957

The orphrey depicts the resurrected
Christ in a mandorla bearing the
banner of the Resurrection on a
cruciform staff. The open tomb
with three fleeing Roman soldiers
is below him and two cherubim are
above. The museum's fragment
consists of a single full repeat with
partial repeats above and below.
For a closely related example, see
Santoro 1981, no. 8.

detail

✳ 10

Orphrey Fragment

Italian (Tuscany); 1450/1500
Lampas: silk
22³/4 x 8 in.
(57.8 x 20.3 cm)
City of Detroit Purchase
(29.281)

Provenance:
Enrico Testa, Florence

Publications:
BDIA, vol. 11, no. 1, 1929, p. 3;
Weibel 1937; Weibel 1952,
no. 208; Markowsky 1976,
p. 141, no. 64

The Virgin sits beneath a portico
with her arms folded over her chest
as the Angel of the Annunciation
appears from the right. A lily is
placed on the tiled floor between
the figures; trees can be seen over a
balustrade behind the angel; a ray of
light and the dove of the Holy Spirit
appears among the clouds in the
sky. Many parallels in this and other
media exist for this design. The
museum's piece consists of two full
repeats and one nearly complete
repeat. For related textiles, see
Karlsruhe 1957, no. 14; Liedholm
1963, p. 41; Markowsky 1976, p. 141,
no. 64; Santoro 1981, no. 3; Milan
1983, no. 35; and Lubin Gallery
[1985].

✳ 11
Orphrey Fragment
Italian (Tuscany); 1450/1500
Lampas: silk and metallic
thread
$42^7/_8$ x $9^3/_8$ in.
(108.8 x 23.7 cm)
City of Detroit Purchase
(29.283)

Provenance:
Enrico Testa, Florence

Publications:
BDIA, vol. 11, no. 1, 1929, p. 3;
Weibel 1937; Weibel 1952,
no. 209

Exhibitions:
Muskegon 1957; Detroit
1978, checklist no. 26

The design shows the Assumption
and Coronation of the Virgin. The
Virgin is seated in the clouds surrounded by angels and cherubim as
God the Father holds a crown over her
head. Below, Saint Thomas kneels
before the open tomb (inscribed
ASV/TAS/ST for "Assumpta est —
She is risen") as he reaches to receive
the holy girdle from the Virgin.

The relic of the Virgin's belt, or holy
girdle, has been in the Tuscan city of
Prato since the twelfth century and it
figures prominently in many Tuscan
works of art.

For related woven orphreys, see
Falke 1936; Fanelli 1981, no. 21;
Cavallo 1986.

✳ 12

Orphrey Fragment
Italian (Tuscany); 1450/1500
Lampas: silk and metallic
thread
16 x 7 in. (40.6 x 17.8 cm)
Founders Society Purchase,
Edsel B. Ford Fund
(31.252)

Provenance:
Josep Gudiol, Vich, Spain

The Annunciation is depicted in a design similar in its major elements to catalogue no. 10, but reversed. The details differ somewhat and the drawing style of this piece is naive in comparison to the other Tuscan woven orphreys in the exhibition. This piece consists of a full repeat that has been stitched to an incomplete length. For stylistically similar pieces, see Markowsky 1976, p. 139, no. 58 and Fanelli 1981, no. 19a.

✳ 13

Panel from an Orphrey
South Netherlandish;
late 15th century
Embroidery: silk and
metallic thread on linen
plain weave
10¹/₈ x 8³/₄ in.
(25.7 x 22.2 cm)
Founders Society Purchase,
Octavia W. Bates and
William Yawkey Funds
(60.45)

Provenance:
Jacob Hirsch, New York;
Adolph Loewi, Los Angeles

Publications:
Weibel 1960-61

Exhibitions:
Grand Rapids 1970

The eight-sided orphrey panel depicts the standing figures of Saint Augustine and his mother Saint Monica, whose names are embroidered in the top border. Augustine, Bishop of Hippo, carries the crozier appropriate to bishops as well as his personal attribute, the heart. He wears the bishop's mitre and a gold cope fastened in front with a morse. Saint Monica is dressed as a nun, holding a heart and a book.

The well-preserved panel is finely embroidered in silk and metallic thread in a style consistent with the late fifteenth century. The attribution to the South Netherlands, however, which the piece has carried since it came to the museum, is less secure. Similar embroideries with the unusual eight-sided shape were

produced in the North Netherlands and in Cologne as well. The Rhine and the Meuse rivers contributed greatly to artistic interchange between these areas and it is often difficult to localize such pieces with certainty on the basis of style alone.

Generally related embroideries are a panel with the Virgin and Child and Saint Willibrord in the Metropolitan Museum of Art in New York (acc. no. 64.101.1385); a panel with the Pietà in the Musées Royaux d'art et d'histoire in Brussels (acc. no. Tx 1360) and a panel of the Nativity (acc. no. Tx 3008) in the same collection; a panel with the Virgin and Child in the Museum Mayer van der Bergh in Antwerp; and the Annunciation in the Schnütgen Museum in Cologne (see Witte 1926).

✳ 14

Dalmatic

Netherlandish embroidery
ca. 1500 on Italian velvet
1450/75
Orphreys: embroidery, silk
and metallic thread on linen
plain weave; velvet: silk and
metallic thread
41 x 44 in.
(104.1 x 111.8 cm)
Gift of Mr. and Mrs. Edgar
B. Whitcomb, Grosse
Pointe, Michigan
(37.56)

Publications:
Weibel 1937a

The crimson and gold velvet that forms the body of the dalmatic is characteristic of Italian weaving of the fifteenth century (see Fanelli 1981, cat. no. 11). It is one of many variations on the pomegranate design which was popular during the fifteenth and sixteenth centuries, particularly in pile-on-pile cut velvets such as this example.

The use of Netherlandish embroidered orphreys on an Italian velvet ground was extremely popular in vestments made around 1500 (see Utrecht 1987 passim). The orphreys in this example were taken from at least two difference sources. The saints in the upper register, for example, appear in a chapel with windows, while all of the others are surmounted by a heavy arcade. The embroidery is somewhat worn throughout and some of the saints' attributes are illegible. The bottom orphreys are all truncated at the lower edge.

15
Shield and Orphreys from a Cope

South Netherlandish;
early 16th century
Embroidery: silk and
metallic thread on linen
plain weave
Shield: 25½ x 22 in.
(64.8 x 55.9 cm)
Orphreys: 43½ x 14¼ in.
each (110.5 x 36.2 cm)
Founders Society Purchase,
Ralph Harman Booth Fund
(61.2)

Provenance:
Duke of Arenberg, Brussels;
Rosenberg and Stiebel,
New York

Publications:
Farcy 1890-1919, vol. 3, pl.
221 and p. 158; Weibel 1962

Exhibitions:
Detroit 1978, checklist no. 22

The two orphrey panels and the shield depict the Seven Sacraments with remarkably accomplished naturalism through the use of the embroidery technique traditionally known as *or nué*. Translated as "shaded gold," the technique uses polychromed silk thread as couching to hide some of the gold in shadow areas and expose it in lighter areas. The large central image on the shield shows the Eucharist before groups of noble laity and distinguished clergy led by the Emperor and the Pope. The scene is set under an elaborately vaulted arcade suggesting the chevet of a great church. The remaining sacraments are shown in smaller architectural enframements suggesting chapels. The sequence of subjects goes from Baptism to Confirmation and Penance on the first panel and continues on the other with Matrimony, Holy Orders, and Extreme Unction.

The theme is rare in surviving textiles of the period, but two extant copes also depict the Seven Sacraments: the cope of Saint-Lieven from the cathedral of Saint Bavo, Ghent, also of the early sixteenth century, and the somewhat earlier cope from the cathedral of Lausanne, now in the Historisches Museum, Bern (Farcy 1890-1919, vol. 1, pl. 72, and vol. 2, pl. 162). Furthermore, there is an important Netherlandish precedent for this conception of the Seven Sacraments in Rogier van der Weyden's *Altarpiece of the Seven Sacraments* in Antwerp (Musée Royal des Beaux-Arts) of 1453/55, where the Eucharist is depicted in the chevet in the center of the triptych, while the other sacraments (depicted in the wings) are administered simultaneously in the side chapels. The orphreys follow the sequence of the Antwerp altarpiece except in reversing the position of Matrimony and Holy Orders.

The embroidery has been removed from the silk damask cope of a later date with which it came to the museum.

✳ 16
Chasuble

Spanish; 16th century
Velvet: silk; Orphrey: embroidery: silk and metallic thread on linen plain weave
47¼ x 26 in.
(120.1 x 66 cm)
Gift of Mrs. C. S. Mott,
Flint, Michigan
(74.296)

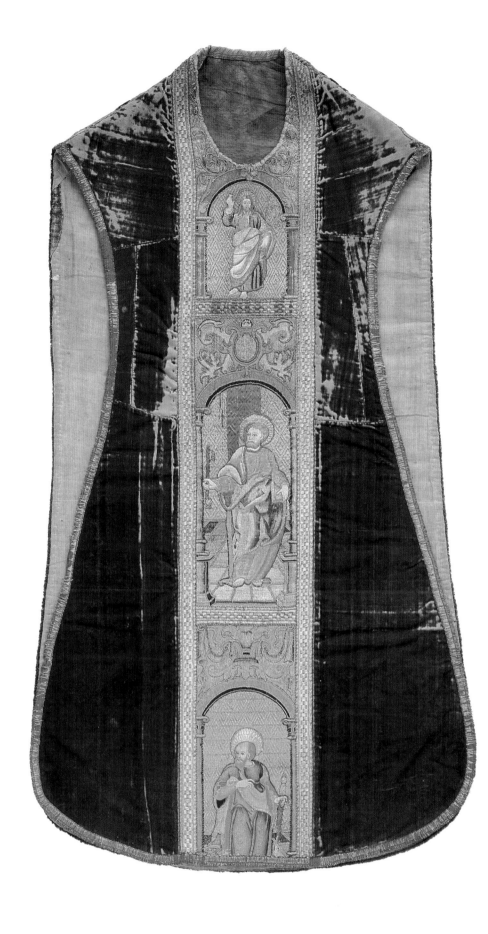

The figures of Christ, Saint Peter, and Saint Paul appear on the embroidered orphrey on the front of this velvet chasuble. On the back are the Virgin and Child, Saint John the Baptist, and Saint Bartholomew. The orphreys are truncated at the bottom, suggesting that they might be originally from another source. The wear and the patches on the velvet suggest that it was not originally used for a chasuble. For generally related Spanish embroideries, see Farcy 1890-1919, vol. 3, pl. 215, and Turmo 1955.

✳ 17

Crucifix

Central European;
16th century
Embroidery: metallic thread
on linen plain weave
28½ x 13 in.
(72.4 x 33 cm)
Founders Society Purchase,
Octavia W. Bates Fund
(48.129)

Provenance:
Leopold Ilké, St. Gall,
Switzerland; F. C. Iklé,
Chicago

This crucifix from the back of
a chasuble, or possibly from an
antependium, is an embroidered
sculpture in low relief. The use of
metallic thread in an embroidery of
this type is highly unusual, but relief
embroidery covered with silk fabric
was popular during the Renaissance
in Germany, Austria, and Bohemia
(see examples in Dreger 1904 and
Drobná 1950, pls. 44, 55, 59).

The zigzag pattern of the ground
cleverly evokes the wood of the cross
while the body of Christ is finely
modelled with raised work. The letters *INRI* inscribed at the top of the
cross and the skull and bones at the
base, both standard elements in crucifixion imagery, were embroidered
separately and applied.

detail

✸ 18

Altar Frontal

Spanish; 1550/80
Embroidery: silk and
metallic thread on linen
plain weave
42¹/₂ x 112 in.
(108 x 284 cm)
Gift of K. T. Keller, Detroit
(37.160)

It is remarkable that this richly embroidered altar frontal which entered the collection in 1937 has never been published. Like the Netherlandish shield and orphreys from a cope (cat. no. 15), this piece is an outstanding example of the technique known as *or nué*. The center of the frontal is occupied by a coat of arms surrounded by the collar of the Order of the Golden Fleece, first used by Charles I of Spain (1500-1558), who became Charles V, Holy Roman Emperor. The same arms were then used by Philip II of Spain from 1556 to 1580, when the arms of Portugal were added. The same arms without those of Portugal, however, were used again during the reigns of Philip IV (1605-1665) and his son Charles III (1661-1700). The heraldic section of the frontal is flanked by two sections of flowering trellis.

The top and side borders depict the Tree of Jesse, beginning with the recumbent Jesse at the lower left, continuing across the top with portrait busts of the ancestors of Christ identified in banderoles, and concluding on the lower right where the Virgin and Child appear. Interspersed among the branches of the Tree of Jesse are seven scenes from the Life of the Virgin. Beginning on the left the scenes are Joachim and Anna at the Golden Gate, the Birth of the Virgin, the Marriage of the Virgin, the Annunciation, the Visitation, the Nativity, and the Presentation in the Temple.

see fold-out on p. 7

✳ **19**

Altar Cover (?)

Swiss; dated 1546
Embroidery: linen on linen
plain weave
68³/₄ x 62¹/₂ in.
(174.6 x 158.8 cm)
Gift of Mrs. John D.
Rockefeller, New York
(24.70)

Publications:
Valentiner 1924

Exhibitions:
Detroit 1978, checklist no. 25

White-on-white linen embroidery, which first became popular in Germany in the twelfth century, persisted well into the sixteenth century in parts of Switzerland and southern Germany (see Trudel 1954). This piece shows the Lamb of God in the central medallion with the inscription *1546 DAS IST DAS LAM GOTTES WELCHES HINMIT DIE SIND DER WELT* ("This is the Lamb of God who takes away the sins of the world"). In the corners are the symbols of the four Evangelists. The remainder of the cover is devoted to flowering branches with a knife, a fork, a fish, and a bird interspersed.

The essentially ecclesiastical nature of the imagery and the inscription recalling the Eucharist suggest that the textile was used as an altar cover. The fish and the utensils, however, evoke a domestic context and it is difficult to be certain how this piece originally functioned. The lace border is a later addition. A similar south German altar cover with the Agnus Dei and the Evangelist symbols is dated 1554 (see Karlsruhe 1986).

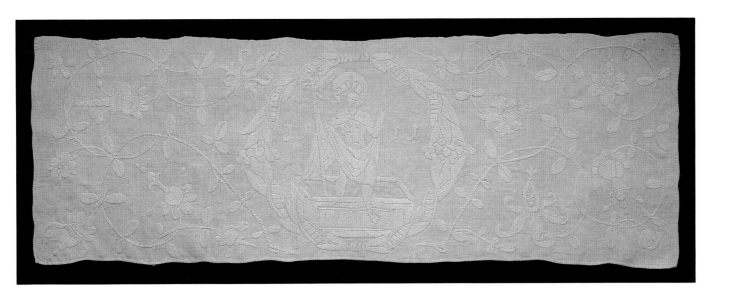

✳ 20
Cover for the Back of a Bench

Swiss; dated 1551
Embroidery: linen on linen
plain weave
15³/₄ x 44¹/₂ in.
(40 x 113 cm)
Founders Society Purchase,
William C. Yawkey Fund
(48.130)

Provenance:
Leopold Iklé, St. Gall,
Switzerland; F. C. Iklé,
Chicago

Publications:
Zurich 1923, no. 271, p. 31

Exhibitions:
Grand Rapids 1970

The Resurrected Christ enclosed
by a wreath stands in the open tomb
carrying a banner, flanked by the
numerals 1551.

✳ 21

Hanging for an Altar or Choirstall

South Netherlandish;
early 16th century
Tapestry: wool and silk
41½ x 93¾ in.
(105.4 x 238.1 cm)
Gift of Mr. and Mrs.
William A. Fisher, Detroit
(49.506)

Exhibitions:
Grand Rapids 1957; Detroit
1978, checklist no. 21

The tapestry depicts the Adoration of the Magi set before a ruined masonry building in a landscape. The seated Virgin and Child are surrounded by the three kings as Saint Joseph looks on from the right. The small size of the tapestry and the horizontal format make it suitable for hanging above a row of choirstalls, as an antependium in front of or a dorsal behind the altar. There are restored areas on both sides of the piece as well as some repair along the ground line at the bottom.

✳ 22
Altar Frontal

South Netherlandish;
1550/1600
Tapestry: wool and silk
44$^{1}/_{2}$ x 101$^{3}/_{4}$ in.
(113 x 258.4 cm)
Gift of K. T. Keller, Detroit
(46.325)

The tapestry depicts the three Theological Virtues in a landscape. Faith, at the left, clasps a book to her chest and a large cross leans on her right shoulder. A small cross can be seen behind her head while a chalice and host rest at her side. In the center Charity holds a flaming heart in her right hand as four children play around her. On the right the winged figure of Hope is seated with a star over her head. She holds tablets with her left hand and an anchor appears behind her feet. According to records in the curatorial file, a nearly identical tapestry was on loan to the Indianapolis Museum of Art until 1985.

In the center of the upper section (or superfrontal) the dove of the Holy Spirit appears in a cartouche. The cartouche is flanked by putti holding ribbons and swags of fruit and foliage. Below the dove is the Tetragrammaton evoking the presence of God the Father. It is composed of the four Hebrew letters transliterated as *JHVH*, which came to be pronounced "Yahweh." The tetragram was popular in the sixteenth century as an alternative to the bearded figure of God the Father. The large cross with Faith at the left evokes the presence of Christ, suggesting an analogy between the Three Virtues and the Trinity.

✳ 23
Stole

Italian; ca. 1600
Velvet: silk
82³/₄ x 8¹/₄ in.
(210.2 x 20.9 cm)
Gift of John Lord Booth,
Grosse Pointe, Michigan
(43.17)

A piece of velvet with a similar
pattern is in Cologne (Markowsky
1976, p. 187, no. 191).

✳ 24
Cope

Italian; ca.1600
Damask: silk; Galloon: silk
and metallic thread
55³/₄ x 116¹/₂ in.
(141.6 x 295.9 cm)
City of Detroit Purchase
(19.158)

Provenance:
Emil Parès, Paris

The silk damasks that make up
the cope and the rectangular patch
date from the late sixteenth or early
seventeenth century. The material
of the orphrey dates from the late
seventeenth century.

detail

✳ 25
Cope

French or Italian; 1710/20
Woven fabric: silk and
metallic thread
115$\frac{1}{2}$ x 56$\frac{1}{2}$ in.
(293.4 x 143.5 cm)
Founders Society Purchase,
Emma S. Fechimer Fund
(67.9)

Provenance:
Orlando Petreni, Florence

So-called bizarre silks of this type
were popular throughout Europe
in the early eighteenth century.
These designs are characterized by
asymmetry and illogic (see Thornton
1965). The large-scale foliage, trumpet
flowers, and other exotic blossoms in
this piece contrast strongly with the
more formal Baroque silk designs of
the seventeenth century, as well as
with the more naturalistic designs of
the 1730s.

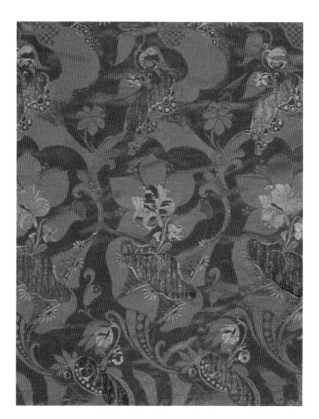

detail

✳ 26
Chasuble and Stole

French; 17/18th century

Brocade: silk and metallic thread on silk plain weave; Galloon: silk and metallic thread

Chasuble: 41¹/₂ x 27¹/₂ in. (105.4 x 69.9 cm)

Stole: 82¹/₂ x 7³/₄ in. (209.6 x 19.7 cm)

Gift of Mrs. Graham John Graham, Bloomfield Hills, Michigan

(50.66.a,.b)

Two distinct fabrics are used in both the chasuble and stole. A seventeenth-century brocade forms the orphrey and ends of the stole; the body of the stole and side panels of the chasuble are a silk of the eighteenth century.

stole not illustrated

✳ 27
Chasuble and Two Stoles
Italian (Venice); early 18th
century
Brocaded damask: silk and
metallic thread
Chasuble (a): 43$\frac{1}{2}$ x 28$\frac{3}{4}$
in. (110.5 x 73 cm)
Stole (b): 46 x 10$\frac{1}{4}$ in.
(116.9 x 26 cm)
Stole (c): 99$\frac{1}{2}$ x 15$\frac{3}{4}$ in.
(252.7 x 40 cm)
Founders Society Purchase,
Emma S. Fechimer Fund
(67.10.a,.b,.c)

Provenance:
Orlando Petreni, Florence

The chasuble and stoles can be
compared to a chasuble in Siena
(Siena 1986).

stoles not illustrated

✳ 28

Dalmatic

Italian; 1730/40
Compound weave: silk and
metallic thread
37¹/₈ x 42¹/₂ in.
(94.3 x 107.9 cm)
Founders Society Purchase,
Octavia W. Bates Fund
(1984.5)

Provenance:
European art market

The design of this silk is an example
of the exuberant, naturalistic style
of the 1730s. The Abegg Stiftung in
Riggisberg, Switzerland, has an
identical dalmatic.

✳ 29

Cope

Italian (Venice); 1730/40
Brocade: silk and metallic
thread on silk satin
113½ x 54¼ in.
(288.3 x 137.8 cm)
Founders Society Purchase
with funds donated to the
Archdiocese of Detroit in
memory of His Eminence,
John Cardinal Dearden,
Archbishop of Detroit,
1958-80
(1989.6)

Provenance:
European art market

Publications:
Santoro [1988?]; *BDIA*, vol.
64, no. 4, 1989, p. 57.

Silks originally woven for secular
purposes were frequently reused for
ecclesiastical vestments. The exclu-
sively military character of the fabric
design of this cope is, however, ex-
traordinary: it includes a crenellated
tower standing on a multi-faceted
fortification. Trees grow on top of the
tower and a flag unfurls at one cor-
ner. At the center of the pattern is a
helmet from which radiate shields
and quivers full of arrows.

The fabric has elements in common
with pieces localized to both Venice
and Lyon. There are some indica-
tions, however, that the fabric

originated in Venice. The white
conical tents visible behind the
tower appear to be of the Turkish
type, recalling the Venetian military
campaign against the Ottoman
Turks of the early eighteenth

century. A similar silk design is
represented in the Detroit Institute
of Arts by a length of fabric with a
pattern of ships at sea (50.185; see
Cavallo 1950-51).

detail

✳ 30
Cope
Italian (Venice?);
mid-18th century
Brocaded damask: silk and
metallic thread
51 x 83 in.
(129.5 x 210.8 cm)
Founders Society Purchase,
Octavia W. Bates Fund
(69.23)

Provenance:
Blumka Gallery, New York

detail

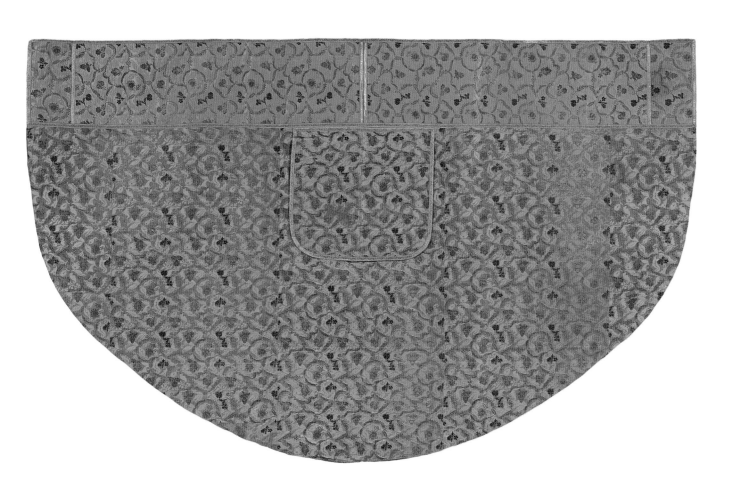

45

✳ 31
Maniple and Stole

Italian (Genoa);
mid-18th century
Velvet: silk and metallic
thread
Maniple: 34$\frac{1}{2}$ x 8$\frac{1}{4}$ in.
(87.6 x 20.9 cm)
Stole: 84 x 9 in.
(213.4 x 22.9 cm)
Gift of Mrs. Emma S.
Fechimer, Detroit
(50.68.a,.b)

The polychromed pattern of this so-
called garden velvet *(velluto giardino)*
is a type usually associated with
Genoa.

stole not illustrated

✳ 32

Chalice Veil

Italian (probably north);
mid-18th century
Embroidery: silk and metallic thread on silk plain
weave moiré
25$\frac{1}{4}$ x 25$\frac{1}{2}$ in.
(64.1 x 64.8 cm)
Gift of Mrs. John Dyar,
Detroit
(25.211)

Richly decorated chalice veils
were an innovation of the sixteenth
century. The church required that
chalice veils be made of silk and
they were often embellished with
gold and silver. The christological
monogram *IHS* in the center of this
example was placed directly over the
chalice and paten until they were
uncovered for the celebration of the
Eucharist.

✱ 33

Textile

Spanish(?); 18/19th century
Plain weave linen with linen
weft loop pile
52¹/₈ x 67⁷/₈ in.
(132.3 x 172.5 cm)
Gift of Mr. and Mrs.
Houston Shields in memory
of Margaret Platter Brown
(69.164)

This enigmatic piece is composed of
two widths of the same linen fabric
sewn together along the selvage,
the bottom section upside down.
The original function of the piece is
unknown, but the complex imagery
is partially ecclesiastical. A pair
of stylized dancing angels flank a
monstrance and a pair of candelabra
on an altar which bears an illegible
inscription. Other elements of this
intriguing design are a portrait
medallion inscribed *A/RA* and a
variety of stylized animals.

✱ 34

Chasuble

French(?); mid-19th century
Embroidery: wool and silk
on linen plain weave canvas
46 x 28 in.
(116.8 x 71.1 cm)
Founders Society Purchase,
Octavia W. Bates Fund,
Emma S. Fechimer Fund,
and William C. Yawkey
Fund
(1988.71)

Provenance:
European art market

Within the large cruciform frame on the back of the chasuble is a closed book, a cross, and the Agnus Dei, or Lamb of God. The floral design of the embroidery is characteristic of western European ornament in the middle of the nineteenth century, making a precise localization difficult without a secure provenance. For a nineteenth-century chasuble embroidered in the same technique, see Chicago 1975, cat. no. 152.

Saints Daniel of Padua and Louis of Toulouse

Late 1490s
Attributed to Jacopo da
Montagnana
Italian (Padua), active
1458-1499(?)
Tempera on panel,
26 x 27 in.
(65.5 x 68 cm)
Gift of Mrs. Ralph Harman
Booth, in memory of her
husband, Ralph Harman
Booth
(43.1)

In this painting from the collection of
the Detroit Institute of Arts, Saint
Louis of Toulouse is in the fore-
ground dressed as a bishop holding
a crozier. He wears a cope with
a jeweled morse and embroidered
orphreys depicting prophets.
Saint Daniel of Padua is on the left
dressed as a deacon. He wears a
dalmatic with the Pietà embroidered
on the orphrey across the chest.
Around his neck is an amice with
an embroidered apparel; a maniple
hangs over his left wrist.

Glossary

Alb: An ankle-length, white linen garment worn by deacons, priests, and bishops under their vestments. It is also worn as the principal garment by acolytes and sub-deacons, etc.

Amice: A rectangular cloth worn around the neck and shoulders by nearly all clergy.

Antependium (altar frontal): A decoration for the front of an altar.

Apparel: A rectangular decorative panel, usually embroidered, used to embellish the alb and the amice.

Bast fiber: A strong, woody fiber obtained chiefly from the stalks of plants. Flax, hemp, and jute are common examples.

Brocade: Specifically, a textile with a supplementary weft that does not cross the entire width of the fabric. Also a general term for a textile with a richly woven pattern.

Burse: A square, pocket-like container for the corporal, or linen cloth used to cover the Eucharistic bread.

Canvas: A coarse cloth woven to form a regular mesh for working with a needle.

Chalice cover (pall or palla): A small, stiff cover placed beneath the chalice veil.

Chalice veil: A square piece of silk fabric used to cover the chalice until the moment of communion.

Chasuble: A long sleeveless vestment worn as the outermost and principal garment by priests during Mass.

Compound weave: A weave in which the weft threads of a selected color are bound on the face of the fabric, while the weft threads of other colors are bound on the reverse side until they are needed for the design.

Cope: A semicircular cloak, worn over the shoulders and fastened in the front by a strip of material or a brooch called a morse. Used by priests and higher clergy as processional, rather than liturgical, garments.

Couching: An embroidery technique in which threads are laid across the surface of the fabric and held in place by stitches of another thread at regular intervals.

Crozier: A staff resembling a shepherd's crook, carried by bishops and abbots as a symbol of office.

Dalmatic: A shin-length tunic with sleeves, worn by deacons as their principal garment and by priests and bishops underneath the chasuble.

Damask: A reversible monochrome fabric in which the background and pattern are distinguished by different weaves.

Embroidery: Ornamentation of a fabric with needlework.

Epitaphios Sindon: Used in the Eastern Church as a cover for the ceremonial bier of Christ from Good Friday until Easter.

Galloon: A band of ribbonlike trim, often of lace or braid with metallic threads.

Ikat: An Indonesian term describing the process of resist-dyeing a pattern on the warp and/or the weft before weaving.

Lampas: A figural weave in which the background is formed by main warps and wefts, while the pattern is formed by weft floats secured by a binding warp.

Lappet: One of two narrow strips of fabric, or streamers, that hang from the back of the mitre.

Lectern cover: A runner used to cover a stand for choir books.

Maniple: A strip of cloth worn over the left forearm by most clergy.

Metallic thread: A term used to describe any thread composed in part or entirely of metallic materials, generally gold or silver. The metal is usually applied to a core of another material.

Mitre: A cap with two points worn by bishops, archbishops, and some abbots.

Moiré: A ribbed fabric with a wavy or watered effect produced by flattening areas, leaving the rest in relief.

Morse: A strip of fabric or a brooch used to fasten a cope in front.

Or nué: Translated as "shaded gold," a technique using polychromed silk thread as couching to hide the gold metallic thread in shaded areas and expose it in lighter areas.

Orphrey: A decorative band applied to chasubles, copes, and dalmatics.

Plain weave (also called **tabby weave**)**:** The simplest weave, in which warps and wefts pass over one another alternately.

Samit (weft-faced compound weave): A weft-patterned weave with complementary wefts in two or more series, usually of different colors, and a main warp and a binding warp. Only one weft thread appears on the face while others are kept to the reverse. The entire surface is covered by weft floats that hide the main warp ends.

Satin weave: A weave in which the weft threads are hidden by more numerous warp threads, or vice versa, resulting in a smooth surface.

Shield: A triangular or shield-shaped piece of cloth at the back of the neck of a cope, developed from the form of a hood.

Stole: A narrow band of cloth worn under the dalmatic or chasuble, hanging down nearly to the ankles.

Tablet weaving: A technique in which the weft threads pass through an opening in the warp (shed) formed by rotating tablets or cards with holes through which the warp threads pass. The technique, executed without a loom, is normally used for narrow bands of fabric.

Tapestry: A variation of plain weave in which colored weft threads are beaten down to completely cover the warp threads. The weft threads do not cross the width of the textile, but are used only where a particular color is required. Also a general term to describe a pictorial hanging.

Velvet: A pile weave produced by a pile warp raised in loops above a ground weave.

>   **cut pile velvet:** Velvet in which the loops are cut to form tufts.

>   **pile on pile velvet:** Velvet in which cut or uncut pile is woven in two or more heights to produce a pattern.

>   **voided velvet:** Velvet in which certain areas of the ground weave are left free from the pile.

Vestment: One of the insignia or ceremonial garments carried or worn by ecclesiastical officiants and assistants as indicative of their rank.

Warp: The threads of a textile that are arranged longitudinally on the loom during weaving.

Weft: The transverse threads that are interwoven with the warp to create fabric.

Weft loop weave: A weave with the weft pulled to form loops on the face of the fabric.

Bibliography and Exhibitions

Aldenkirchen 1884
Aldenkirchen, J., "Früh-mittelalterliche Leinen-Stickereien," *Jahrbücher des Vereins von Alterthums-Freuden im Rheinlande*, vol. 78, Bonn, 1884, pp. 256-72 and plates.

Battiscombe 1956
Battiscombe, C. F.,ed; *Relics of Saint Cuthbert*, Oxford University Press, 1956, pp. 433-52.

BDIA
Bulletin of the Detroit Institute of Arts.

Braun 1907
Braun, Joseph, *Die Liturgische Gewandung im Occident und Orient*, Freiburg im Breisgau, Herdersche Verlagshandlung, 1907.

Burnham 1980
Burnham, Dorothy K., *Warp and Weft: A Dictionary of Textile Terms*, New York, Charles Scribner's Sons, 1980.

Cavallo 1950-51
Cavallo, A. S., "A Venetian Brocaded Satin of the 18th Century," *Bulletin of the Detroit Institute of Arts*, vol. 30, 1950-51, pp. 68-70.

Cavallo 1967
Cavallo, Adolph S., *Tapestries of Europe and of Colonial Peru in the Museum of Fine Arts, Boston* (2 vols.), Boston, Museum of Fine Arts, 1967.

Cavallo 1986
Cavallo, Adolph S. *Textiles: Isabella Stewart Gardner Museum*, Boston, Isabella Stewart Gardner Museum, 1986, no. 122.

Chicago 1975
Chicago, Art Institute of Chicago, *Raiment for the Lord's Service: A Thousand Years of Western Vestments*, exh. cat. by Christa C. Mayer-Thurman, 1975.

Cleveland 1985
Cleveland, Cleveland Museum of Art, *Textiles in Daily Life in the Middle Ages;* exh. cat. by Rebecca Martin, 1985.

Collingwood 1982
Collingwood, Peter, *The Techniques of Tablet Weaving*, New York, Watson-Guptill Publications, 1982, pp. 346-49.

Cologne 1978
Cologne, Schnütgen Museum, *Die Parler und der Schöne Stil: 1350-1400*, exh. cat. edited by Anton Legner, 1978 (3 vols.).

Cranbrook 1965
Cranbrook Academy of Art, Bloomfield Hills, Michigan, "Ornamentation: The Art of Fabric Decoration," 1965.

Detroit 1978
Detroit Institute of Arts, "Textile Masterpieces from the Detroit Institute of Arts," September 13, 1978 – January 14, 1979.

Dreger 1904
Dreger, Moriz, *Künstlerische Entwicklung der Weberei und Stickerei* (2 vols.), Vienna, K. K. Hof- und Staatsdruckerei, 1904, vol. 2, pl. 195.

Drobná 1950
Drobná, Zoroslava, *Les trésors de la broderie religieuse en Tschecoslovaquie*, Prague, Sfinx, 1950 (orig. 1949).

Einhorn 1971
Einhorn, J. W., "Ein jungst aufgefundenes Fragment der Soester Lesepult-Decke im Victoria and Albert Museum London," *Zeitschrift für Kunstgeschichte*, vol. 34, no. 1, 1971, pp. 47-58.

Einhorn 1976
Einhorn, J. W., *Spiritalis Unicornis: Das Einhorn als Bedeutungsträger in Literatur und Kunst des Mittelalters* (Münsterische Mittelalter-Schriften, vol. 13), Munich, Wilhelm Fink Verlag, 1976, p. 354.

Falke 1936
Falke, Otto von, *Decorative Silks*, New York, William Helburn, 1936 (3rd ed.), fig. 475.

Fanelli 1981
Fanelli, Rosalia Bonito, *Five Centuries of Italian Textiles: 1300-1800, A Selection from the Museo del Tessuto Prato*, exh. cat., Florence, 1981.

Farcy 1890-1919
Farcy, Louis de, *La Broderie du XIe Siècle jusqu'à nos jours* (3 vols.), Angers, Belhomme, 1890-1919.

Florence 1990
Florence, Museo Nazionale del Bargello, *Bordi figurati del Rinascimento*, exh. cat. by Paolo Peri, 1990.

Gräbke 1938
Gräbke, H. A., "Eine westfälische Gruppe gestickter Leinendecken des Mittelalters," *Westfalen*, vol. 23, no. 3, 1938, pp. 179-194, pls. 38-46.

Grand Rapids 1957
Grand Rapids Art Gallery, Christmas Exhibition, December 5, 1956 – January 6, 1957.

Grand Rapids 1970
Grand Rapids Art Museum, "Magic of Fibers," April 5 – May 3, 1970.

Gurdus 1969
Gurdus, Luba, "The Newly Discovered Epitaphios Designed by Christopher Zafarociv," *Bulletin of the Needle and Bobbin Club*, vol. 52, 1969, pp. 3-25.

Hulst 1960
Hulst, Roger-A. d', et al., *Tapisseries flammandes du XIVe au XVIIIe siècle*, Brussels, Editions Arcade, 1960.

Husband 1971
Husband, Timothy B., et al.; "Ecclesiastical Vestments of the Middle Ages: An Exhibition," *The Metropolitan Museum of Art Bulletin*, vol. 29, no. 7, 1971, pp. 285-317.

Jaques [1953]
Jaques, Renate, *Deutsche Textilkunst*, Krefeld, Scherpe-Verlag, [1953].

Johnstone 1967
Johnstone, Pauline, *The Byzantine Tradition in Church Embroidery*, London, Alec Tiranti, 1967.

Karlsruhe 1957
Badisches Landesmuseums Karlsruhe, *Alte Textilien*, Karlsruhe, 1957.

Karlsruhe 1986
Badisches Landesmuseum, Karlsruhe, *Die Renaissance im deutschen südwesten*, exh. cat. (2 vols.), 1986, vol. 2, cat. Q17, pp. 819-20.

Kende Galleries 1945
Kende Galleries, New York, sales cat., April 19-20, 1945.

Liedholm 1963
Liedholm, Alf, *Textilmönstrets Historia*, Stockholm, Esselte, 1963.

Los Angeles 1944
Los Angeles County Museum of Art, Cleveland Museum of Art, and the Detroit Institute of Arts, *Two Thousand Years of Silk Weaving*, exh. cat., New York, E. Weyhe, 1944.

Lubin Gallery [1985]
Edward R. Lubin: European Works of Art, A Selection from the Gallery, New York, [1985], no. 40.

Ludorff 1899
Ludorff, A., *Die Bau- und Kunstdenkmäler von Westfalen (Die Bau- und Kunstdenkmäler des Kreises Paderborn)*, Münster, Kommissions Verlag, 1899, p. 140 and pl. 110.

Markowsky 1976
Markowsky, Barbara, *Europäische Seidengewebe des 13.-18. Jahrhunderts*, Cologne, Kunstgewerbemuseum der Stadt Köln, 1976.